PRINCEWILL LAGANG

Dating Differently: A Christian Approach

First published by PRINCEWILL LAGANG 2023

Copyright © 2023 by Princewill Lagang

All rights reserved. No part of this publication may be reproduced, stored or transmitted in any form or by any means, electronic, mechanical, photocopying, recording, scanning, or otherwise without written permission from the publisher. It is illegal to copy this book, post it to a website, or distribute it by any other means without permission.

Princewill Lagang asserts the moral right to be identified as the author of this work.

First edition

This book was professionally typeset on Reedsy.
Find out more at reedsy.com

Contents

1	The Foundation of Christian Dating	1
2	The Search for a God-Centered Partner	4
3	Building a Strong Foundation for a God-Centered Relationship	7
4	The Unique Challenges and Joys of Dating Differently	10
5	Navigating Life Together - Decision-Making, Dreams, and...	13
6	A Love that Endures - Grace and Inspiration	16
7	Reflection, Transformation, and Hope	19
8	Embracing the Journey	22
9	Walking in Faith, Love, and Grace	25
10	A Legacy of Love and Faith	28
11	A Love That Never Fades	31
12	Forever Faithful	34

1

The Foundation of Christian Dating

Title: Dating Differently: A Christian Approach

The sun hung low in the evening sky, casting a warm, golden glow over the small town of Graceville. Nestled in the heart of the Bible Belt, it was a place where traditional values and close-knit communities thrived. As the church bells rang out their gentle invitation, a group of young adults gathered in the cozy basement of the Graceville Community Church. They had come with open hearts, seeking to explore a path less traveled in the world of dating: a Christian approach.

In an age where dating often seemed like a minefield of uncertainty, confusion, and heartache, these young individuals were determined to follow a different set of principles – the timeless teachings of their Christian faith. They were eager to embark on a journey that would lead to deeper connections, lasting relationships, and, above all, a love that was rooted in their shared spirituality.

This chapter will lay the foundation for their pursuit, unraveling the principles that define Christian dating and examining the reasons behind choosing this path. Let us explore the core values that guide this unique approach to romance and relationships.

1.1. The Power of Faith

The concept of faith is central to the Christian approach to dating. In a world that often champions the superficial and fleeting, Christians believe that faith in God can guide their decisions, not only in matters of spirituality but also in matters of the heart. As they gathered in the basement of the Graceville Community Church, they were reminded of a verse from Proverbs 3:5-6: "Trust in the Lord with all your heart and lean not on your own understanding; in all your ways submit to him, and he will make your paths straight."

This trust in the divine plan offered them a sense of reassurance in their pursuit of love. They believed that, by surrendering their hearts to God's guidance, they would find the strength to navigate the complexities of dating with grace, patience, and wisdom.

1.2. The Importance of Purity

Purity was another key principle shaping the Christian approach to dating. In a culture often saturated with casual relationships and hook-up culture, these young adults sought a different path. Their belief in purity was not merely about abstinence from physical intimacy before marriage, but it was also a commitment to emotional purity. They aimed to maintain a purity of heart and mind, avoiding games, manipulation, and deceit.

As one of the group members, Sarah, expressed, "Purity is not just about avoiding physical sin; it's about guarding your heart and ensuring that your motives are rooted in love and respect."

1.3. The Sanctity of Marriage

Christian dating was ultimately guided by the belief in the sanctity of marriage. For these young individuals, dating was not a frivolous pursuit but a purposeful journey towards a lifelong commitment. Marriage was seen as a sacred covenant before God, and the dating process was intended to be a preparation for this lifelong partnership.

As John, another member of the group, explained, "Our aim is not just to find someone to date; it's to find someone to share a lifetime with, someone with whom we can grow spiritually and emotionally."

1.4. The Support of Community

One of the unique aspects of the Christian approach to dating was the emphasis on community support. The group in Graceville was not navigating this journey alone. They leaned on the wisdom and guidance of their church family, pastors, and mentors who had walked a similar path. This support system provided them with encouragement, accountability, and a shared vision of what Christian dating could be.

The members of the Graceville Community Church had embarked on a journey that was countercultural, one that required a deep and abiding faith in God's plan, a commitment to purity, a dedication to the sanctity of marriage, and the support of their Christian community. They believed that by dating differently, they could build lasting relationships that mirrored the love and grace they had found in their faith.

In the chapters to come, we will delve deeper into the practical aspects of Christian dating, exploring topics such as finding the right partner, building a strong foundation, and navigating challenges along the way. We will continue to unpack the principles that guide this unique approach, shedding light on the power of faith, the importance of purity, and the sanctity of marriage that define dating differently through a Christian lens.

2

The Search for a God-Centered Partner

Title: Dating Differently: A Christian Approach

The basement of the Graceville Community Church hummed with anticipation as the group of young adults gathered for another meeting on their journey of Christian dating. As they took their seats and opened their Bibles, they were eager to explore a fundamental aspect of dating differently: the search for a God-centered partner.

2.1. Defining the God-Centered Relationship

To these young Christians, a God-centered relationship was more than just a superficial connection. It was a profound bond that went beyond shared interests or physical attraction. It was built on a foundation of faith, love, and a shared commitment to walk with God together.

A member of the group, David, shared his perspective: "In a God-centered relationship, our faith is not an accessory, but the core of our connection. We strive to encourage each other in our spiritual journeys and support one another in our walk with God."

2.2. Seeking Compatibility in Faith

The search for a God-centered partner began with a fundamental question: "Is our faith compatible?" While it was essential to respect and appreciate differences in theology or religious practices, they recognized that a shared faith foundation was the cornerstone of a lasting relationship.

Megan, another member, reflected on this, saying, "Our faith is our compass. It guides our decisions, values, and priorities. When you're in a relationship with someone who shares that same compass, it makes the journey more aligned and harmonious."

2.3. The Role of Prayer

For these Christian daters, prayer was not only a tool for personal guidance but also a vital part of their search for a partner. They believed in the power of prayer to lead them to someone who shared their values, vision, and faith. Each member of the group committed to praying earnestly for wisdom and discernment in their pursuit of love.

Prayer was not just about asking, but also about listening. Sarah said, "We don't just list our preferences to God; we also listen to His nudges and guidance. It's a conversation, a partnership, even in our search for the right person."

2.4. Navigating the Modern Dating Scene

The Christian approach to dating was not an escape from the challenges of modern dating but a unique way to navigate it. In a world filled with dating apps, casual encounters, and societal pressures, they recognized the need to remain true to their faith values.

The group discussed practical tips for dating differently in the modern world, including setting healthy boundaries, being open and honest in communication, and maintaining accountability within their Christian community.

2.5. The Patience of Waiting

Patience was a virtue that held a special place in their journey of finding a God-centered partner. They understood that God's timing might not align with their desires and that waiting for the right person was a test of their faith and trust in His plan.

John shared his thoughts on patience: "Sometimes, we may feel lonely or discouraged in the waiting, but we believe that God is preparing us and our future partner for something beautiful. It's about trusting in His timing."

As the meeting concluded, the group members left the basement with a renewed commitment to seeking a God-centered partner. They understood that the search might be challenging, but they were convinced that their approach was rooted in the principles of their Christian faith. In the next chapter, they would explore how to build a strong foundation for a God-centered relationship, discussing topics like communication, shared values, and nurturing spiritual growth in their partners and themselves.

3

Building a Strong Foundation for a God-Centered Relationship

Title: Dating Differently: A Christian Approach

In the heart of Graceville, where the leaves of ancient oaks whispered secrets and the community church stood as a sentinel of faith, the group of young Christians continued their journey of dating differently. The previous chapters had focused on the principles of Christian dating, including the search for a God-centered partner. Now, they were ready to dive into the core of their relationships – building a strong foundation.

3.1. Effective Communication

For these young Christians, communication was more than just talking; it was the key to building trust and understanding. They recognized the importance of honest and open conversations in a God-centered relationship.

Beth, one of the group members, shared her perspective: "Effective communication allows us to share our thoughts, feelings, and, most importantly, our faith journey. It's about being there for each other, listening, and empathizing."

3.2. Shared Values and Priorities

A God-centered relationship was built upon a common set of values and priorities. These values included faith, family, service, and a commitment to living out their Christian beliefs.

Tom, a member of the group, explained, "When we share core values, it becomes easier to make important life decisions together. We can prioritize our faith and service to God as a couple."

3.3. Growing Together Spiritually

In a God-centered relationship, spiritual growth was not a solitary pursuit but a shared journey. The group emphasized the importance of nurturing each other's faith and fostering spiritual growth.

Megan expressed her belief in this, saying, "We read the Bible together, pray together, and attend church services as a couple. Our relationship is a sanctuary for spiritual growth, a place where we encourage each other to draw closer to God."

3.4. Overcoming Challenges

The group members recognized that every relationship faced challenges. For them, facing challenges was an opportunity to grow in their faith and as a couple. They believed that the way they dealt with difficulties could strengthen their bond.

David explained, "Challenges can either tear us apart or bring us closer. We choose to approach them with prayer, patience, and a shared commitment to working through them."

3.5. Accountability and Support

Accountability within their Christian community played a significant role in building a strong foundation. The group understood that their relationship was not isolated but connected to the larger faith community.

Sarah shared her thoughts on this: "Our friends, mentors, and church family hold us accountable, providing guidance and wisdom when we need it. It's a support system that ensures we stay on the right path."

As the meeting concluded, the group left with a deeper understanding of how to build a strong foundation for a God-centered relationship. They knew that their approach to dating was not without its challenges, but it was rooted in their unwavering faith and commitment to a shared journey with God at its center.

In the next chapter, they would explore the unique challenges and joys of dating differently through a Christian lens. They would discuss the beauty of a love that was grounded in faith and the fulfillment they found in their distinctive approach to relationships.

4

The Unique Challenges and Joys of Dating Differently

Title: Dating Differently: A Christian Approach

In the heart of Graceville, where faith, community, and love intersected, the group of young Christians gathered for another session of their journey into dating differently. The previous chapters had illuminated the principles and practices of a God-centered relationship. Now, they were ready to explore the unique challenges and joys that came with their Christian approach to dating.

4.1. Challenges of Dating Differently

4.1.1. Cultural Pressures

Dating differently often meant swimming against the cultural tide. The group members shared their experiences of encountering skepticism and misunderstanding from friends and family who didn't understand their faith-based approach.

Emily, a member of the group, spoke of this challenge: "There are moments when it feels like we're swimming against the current. People wonder why we don't just go with the flow, but we're anchored in our faith."

4.1.2. Patience and Waiting

One of the unique challenges of Christian dating was the need for patience and waiting for the right person. The group recognized that God's timing might not align with their desires, and waiting for the right partner was a test of their faith and trust in His plan.

Tom shared his thoughts on patience: "It can be hard to wait, especially when loneliness or societal pressures creep in. But we hold onto our faith and trust that God has something wonderful in store for us."

4.1.3. Accountability

While the support of their Christian community was invaluable, it also came with a level of accountability. Members acknowledged that this could be challenging at times, as they were answerable not only to themselves but to their faith community.

Megan spoke about accountability: "It can be a bit intimidating, knowing that your relationship is under the watchful eyes of the community. But it keeps us honest, and it's a beautiful aspect of dating differently."

4.2. Joys of Dating Differently

4.2.1. Deeper Spiritual Connection

The group members spoke of the profound joy in sharing a deep spiritual connection with their partners. They found that their faith was not just a common interest but the binding force that strengthened their relationship.

David expressed, "There's a unique joy in sharing the deepest parts of our hearts and souls. Our faith is the tie that binds us, and it creates a profound connection."

4.2.2. A Sense of Purpose

Dating differently through a Christian lens brought a sense of purpose and intention to their relationships. They understood that their love was not just about personal happiness but about serving God together.

Beth said, "Our love has a purpose – to glorify God and serve others. It gives our relationship a sense of direction and fulfillment."

4.2.3. Supportive Community

The joy of having a supportive community was a recurring theme. The group emphasized how their faith community provided encouragement, guidance, and a sense of belonging that enriched their journey.

Sarah reflected on this joy: "Our friends, mentors, and church family are our cheerleaders. They celebrate our love, guide us, and remind us that we're not alone on this path."

As the meeting concluded, the group members left with a deeper appreciation for the challenges and joys of dating differently through a Christian approach. They knew that their journey was a unique one, guided by faith, commitment, and a love that was deeply rooted in their spirituality.

In the next chapter, they would explore the practical aspects of maintaining a God-centered relationship and navigating the complexities of life together, from making important decisions to supporting each other's dreams and aspirations.

5

Navigating Life Together - Decision-Making, Dreams, and Aspirations

Title: Dating Differently: A Christian Approach

In the heart of Graceville, where faith was the compass for love, the group of young Christians gathered once more to delve into the practical aspects of dating differently. The previous chapters had illuminated the principles, foundations, and unique challenges and joys of their Christian approach to dating. Now, they were ready to explore how to navigate life together in a God-centered relationship.

5.1. Making Important Decisions

For these young Christians, making important life decisions was a shared endeavor. They recognized that their faith was not just a part of their lives but a guiding force in their decision-making.

Emily, a member of the group, shared her perspective: "Our faith informs our choices. Whether it's our career paths, where we want to live, or even how we want to raise a family, we seek God's guidance in every decision."

5.2. Supporting Each Other's Dreams

In a God-centered relationship, they emphasized the importance of supporting each other's dreams and aspirations. They believed that their love should be a source of encouragement for their partners to pursue their passions and dreams.

Tom expressed this sentiment: "We believe in each other's potential. Our love isn't possessive but empowering. We're there to cheer each other on and to see each other fulfill our God-given potential."

5.3. Fostering Spiritual Growth

Nurturing spiritual growth remained at the core of their relationships. They emphasized the importance of challenging each other to grow in their faith, as well as growing together as a couple.

Megan spoke about the role of spiritual growth: "Our love doesn't stagnate; it evolves with our spiritual journeys. We read, learn, and pray together, and we're there to lift each other up in times of spiritual challenge."

5.4. Handling Challenges Together

Challenges were inevitable in life, and they recognized that handling them together required faith, patience, and a shared commitment to support each other through difficult times.

David reflected on this: "Challenges can be tough, but they're opportunities for our faith to shine. We face them together, knowing that we're stronger as a couple."

5.5. Seeking God's Guidance

In all aspects of life, they remained committed to seeking God's guidance. They believed that God's wisdom and direction were essential for a life lived in alignment with their faith.

Beth shared her thoughts on seeking God's guidance: "We pray together, individually, and as a couple. We seek God's will in all we do, and it brings a sense of peace and confidence to our journey."

As the meeting concluded, the group members left with a deeper understanding of how to navigate life together in a God-centered relationship. They knew that their approach was not without its challenges, but it was grounded in their unwavering faith and commitment to building a life that honored God.

In the next chapter, they would explore the beauty of a love that was enduring, filled with grace, and a source of inspiration to others who sought to date differently through a Christian lens.

6

A Love that Endures - Grace and Inspiration

Title: Dating Differently: A Christian Approach

In the heart of Graceville, where love was nurtured with faith and community, the group of young Christians gathered once more to explore the depth of their Christian approach to dating. They had discussed the principles, foundations, challenges, joys, and practical aspects of their relationships. Now, they were ready to delve into the beauty of a love that endures, filled with grace and inspiration.

6.1. A Love that Endures

For these young Christians, their relationships were not built on fleeting emotions or temporary infatuations. They believed in a love that was enduring, rooted in their shared faith and commitment to each other.

Emily expressed this enduring love: "Our love isn't here today and gone tomorrow. It's a love that endures through the trials and joys of life, and it's a reflection of God's enduring love for us."

6.2. Grace in Relationships

The concept of grace played a significant role in their relationships. They understood that grace was essential for forgiving each other's flaws and mistakes, and for providing the compassion and patience that their partners deserved.

Tom shared his thoughts on grace: "We don't hold onto grudges or past mistakes. We offer grace to each other, just as God offers it to us. It's a cornerstone of our relationship."

6.3. A Source of Inspiration

In dating differently through a Christian lens, they aimed to be a source of inspiration to others. Their love was not just a personal matter but a testament to the beauty of faith-based relationships.

Megan expressed their desire to inspire others: "We want our love to be an example, a source of hope and inspiration to those who may be seeking a different, more meaningful way to love."

6.4. A Love that Serves

Their love was rooted in a desire to serve not only each other but also their community and the world. They believed that their relationship had a purpose greater than personal happiness.

David spoke about their service-oriented love: "We seek to serve others, just as Jesus served. Our love isn't insular; it's a vessel for God's love to flow through us and touch those around us."

6.5. The Role of Community

Their Christian community played a significant role in fostering enduring love. They leaned on the wisdom, support, and encouragement of their faith community to help strengthen their relationships.

Beth expressed their gratitude for community support: "Our friends, mentors, and church family are pillars of strength. They remind us of the importance of enduring love and offer guidance when we need it."

As the meeting concluded, the group members left with a deeper understanding of the enduring love that their Christian approach to dating had brought into their lives. They knew that their approach was not without its challenges, but it was grounded in their unwavering faith and commitment to building relationships that reflected God's enduring love.

In the final chapter, they would reflect on their journey, the transformation it had brought to their lives, and their hope for a future filled with love and purpose.

7

Reflection, Transformation, and Hope

Title: Dating Differently: A Christian Approach

In the heart of Graceville, where faith and love intertwined, the group of young Christians gathered for their final session on their journey of dating differently. The preceding chapters had explored the principles, foundations, challenges, joys, and enduring nature of their Christian approach to dating. Now, it was time to reflect on their journey, the transformation it had brought into their lives, and their hope for the future.

7.1. Reflection on the Journey

As they looked back on their journey of dating differently through a Christian lens, the group members felt a deep sense of gratitude. They reflected on the spiritual growth, the deepening of their faith, and the connections they had formed.

Emily shared her reflections: "Our journey has been transformative. We've seen our love and faith grow, and we've formed bonds with each other and our faith community that are unbreakable."

7.2. Transformation through Faith

Their Christian approach to dating had transformed their lives. They spoke of how their relationships had become vehicles for spiritual growth, shaping them into better versions of themselves.

Tom shared his thoughts on transformation: "Our faith has become the bedrock of our relationships, and that has transformed us in profound ways. We've become more patient, more compassionate, and more rooted in our beliefs."

7.3. Hope for the Future

Looking to the future, the group members were filled with hope. They believed that their approach to dating was a foundation for a lifetime of love, faith, and purpose.

Megan expressed their hope for the future: "We hope to continue nurturing our love, our faith, and our service to others. Our future is bright because it's filled with love that endures."

7.4. A Message to Others

Before concluding their final session, the group members had a message for those who might be considering a Christian approach to dating. They encouraged others to explore this path, emphasizing the transformative power of faith and enduring love.

David shared their message: "To those who are seeking a different way to date, we want to say that it's a beautiful journey. It's a path filled with grace, purpose, and the enduring love of God. We hope you'll find the same joy and fulfillment we have."

7.5. A Life Rooted in Faith

As they left the basement of the Graceville Community Church, the group members were filled with gratitude for their journey of dating differently through a Christian approach. Their lives were now rooted in faith, their relationships were enduring, and they looked to the future with hope.

Their journey was a testament to the power of faith in shaping relationships that were grounded in love, grace, and a shared commitment to God. In their walk of faith and love, they hoped to continue inspiring others to embrace a similar path, one that promised a future of enduring, transformative love.

8

Embracing the Journey

Title: Dating Differently: A Christian Approach

In the heart of Graceville, where love was intertwined with faith and community, the group of young Christians had walked a unique path in their journey of dating differently. The preceding chapters had explored the principles, foundations, challenges, joys, the enduring nature of their Christian approach, and their reflections on the journey. Now, it was time to reflect on the lessons learned and the wisdom gained as they embraced the journey.

8.1. Lessons Learned

As they looked back on their journey, the group members recognized the invaluable lessons they had learned. Their Christian approach to dating had provided a wealth of insights into love, faith, and relationships.

Emily shared some of the lessons they had gained: "We've learned the power of faith in guiding our decisions and deepening our love. We've learned the importance of patience, forgiveness, and grace in our relationships. And we've learned that our love can be a source of inspiration and service to others."

8.2. Wisdom Gained

The journey of dating differently had also bestowed wisdom upon them. They had grown wiser in their understanding of the complexities of love and the significance of a faith-centered approach to relationships.

Tom reflected on the wisdom gained: "We've gained a deep well of wisdom about what it means to love and be loved. We've learned that love is not just a feeling but a commitment. We've also found that a faith-centered approach to dating brings a level of depth and meaning to our relationships that we wouldn't trade for anything."

8.3. Embracing the Journey

As they embraced the journey and looked ahead, the group members acknowledged that their path was a continuous one. They understood that the principles of faith, purity, and a commitment to a God-centered relationship were not static but dynamic and evolving.

Megan shared her perspective on embracing the journey: "Our journey is ongoing. We're committed to growing in faith, deepening our love, and continuing to inspire others. It's not just about reaching a destination; it's about the beauty of the journey itself."

8.4. Inspiring Others

One of their primary goals was to inspire others to explore a similar path of dating differently through a Christian lens. They believed that their journey could serve as a beacon of hope and encouragement for those seeking a more meaningful way to love.

David expressed their hope to inspire others: "We want to be a source of inspiration for anyone who might be considering a Christian approach to dating. We hope our journey can shine a light on a path that is filled with faith, love, and grace."

8.5. A Future of Hope

As they left the basement of the Graceville Community Church, the group members were filled with hope for the future. Their journey of dating differently had transformed their lives, and they looked forward to a future rooted in faith, enduring love, and the joy of inspiring others.

Their path was a testament to the beauty of a Christian approach to dating, one that brought depth, purpose, and a unique connection to God and each other. As they continued their journey, they were committed to embracing the challenges and joys that lay ahead, guided by their unwavering faith and the enduring love they had discovered.

9

Walking in Faith, Love, and Grace

Title: Dating Differently: A Christian Approach

In the heart of Graceville, where the community church stood as a symbol of faith and love, the group of young Christians had journeyed through the principles, foundations, challenges, joys, and reflections on their Christian approach to dating. As they gathered for the final chapter of their exploration, they looked forward to walking in faith, love, and grace as they continued their journey.

9.1. A Lifetime of Faith

For these young Christians, faith was not just a part of their relationships; it was a guiding force that would lead them throughout their lives. They recognized that their faith would continue to shape their decisions, values, and priorities in the years to come.

Emily spoke about the significance of faith: "Our faith is not a temporary aspect of our lives. It's a lifelong journey. We know that we'll keep trusting in God's plan, drawing closer to Him, and allowing our faith to guide us."

9.2. Enduring Love

Their love was enduring, rooted in their shared faith and commitment to each other. They acknowledged that their enduring love was a testament to their faith and the depth of their relationship.

Tom expressed their enduring love: "We're not just in this for the short term. We're committed to a love that will last a lifetime. It's a love that endures through the seasons of life."

9.3. Embracing Grace

Grace remained a cornerstone of their relationships. They understood that offering grace to each other, as well as seeking God's grace in their own lives, was a continuous practice that would help sustain their love.

Megan shared her thoughts on embracing grace: "We'll keep extending grace to one another, recognizing that we all have imperfections. We'll also embrace the grace of God in our lives, knowing that it sustains us."

9.4. The Joy of Service

Their Christian approach to dating had instilled in them a sense of purpose and service. They believed that their relationship was not just about their own happiness but about serving others and glorifying God.

David spoke about the joy of service: "Our relationship is a vessel for service and love. We'll continue to serve our community and be a source of love and inspiration to those around us."

9.5. Inspiring Others

As they looked ahead, the group members were determined to inspire others. They hoped that their journey would serve as a beacon of hope for those who sought to date differently through a Christian lens.

Beth expressed their hope to inspire others: "Our journey isn't just about us. We hope that it can inspire others to explore a faith-centered approach to dating and to find the same joy, purpose, and enduring love we've discovered."

As they concluded their final session, the group members left with a deep sense of faith, love, and grace. Their journey was a testament to the beauty of a Christian approach to dating, one that offered a lifelong path filled with depth, purpose, and a unique connection to God and each other.

With faith as their compass, enduring love as their guide, and grace as their foundation, they were prepared to continue their journey, walking together in faith, love, and grace, forever.

10

A Legacy of Love and Faith

Title: Dating Differently: A Christian Approach

In the heart of Graceville, where the community church stood as a beacon of faith, the group of young Christians had completed their exploration of a Christian approach to dating. As they gathered for their final chapter, they were ready to reflect on the legacy of love and faith they hoped to leave behind.

10.1. The Legacy of Love

For these young Christians, love was not just a personal emotion but a legacy they wished to pass on to the generations that would follow. They believed that their enduring love would serve as an example for their children and grandchildren.

Emily spoke of the legacy of love: "Our love isn't just for us. We hope that our children and their children will see the depth of our love and be inspired to pursue relationships rooted in faith, commitment, and enduring love."

10.2. The Power of Faith

Faith was a core part of their legacy. They recognized that their unwavering trust in God's plan would be a source of inspiration for those who looked to them for guidance.

Tom expressed the power of faith in their legacy: "We want to leave a legacy of faith, to show that a life anchored in faith is a life of purpose, direction, and profound love."

10.3. Inspiring Future Generations

The group members were committed to inspiring future generations to explore a Christian approach to dating. They believed that their journey could offer hope and encouragement to others who sought a different way to love.

Megan shared her thoughts on inspiring future generations: "We want to be an inspiration, to show that dating differently through a Christian lens is not only possible but profoundly beautiful. We hope our journey can inspire others to seek the same."

10.4. A Life of Service

Their legacy extended beyond their relationships; it was a life of service that they aimed to pass on. They hoped that their commitment to service and love would inspire others to make a positive impact on the world.

David spoke of their legacy of service: "Our relationship is a vessel for service, and we hope to inspire others to serve their communities and make the world a better place."

10.5. The Enduring Impact

As they concluded their final chapter, the group members were filled with a sense of purpose. Their journey of dating differently through a Christian approach had left an enduring impact on their lives and relationships.

Beth summed up their feelings: "We're grateful for the legacy of love and faith we've been building. It's a testament to the beauty of a faith-centered approach to dating, one that leaves a lasting mark on the world."

With love as their legacy, faith as their foundation, and a commitment to service, the group of young Christians left their meeting, ready to continue their journey with the hope of inspiring others to date differently, through a Christian lens, and to build a legacy of love and faith for generations to come.

11

A Love That Never Fades

Title: Dating Differently: A Christian Approach

In the heart of Graceville, where faith and love were the guiding forces, the group of young Christians had embarked on a profound journey of dating differently. Their exploration had covered the principles, foundations, challenges, joys, reflections, and the legacy of their Christian approach to dating. As they gathered for the final chapter, they contemplated a love that would never fade.

11.1. A Love That Endures

For these young Christians, the love they had nurtured was not just enduring; it was a love that they believed would never fade. They understood that their faith, commitment, and enduring love formed a bond that was unbreakable.

Emily expressed this unwavering love: "Our love is not here today and gone tomorrow. It's a love that grows stronger with each passing day, a love that will stand the test of time."

11.2. The Role of Faith

Their love was deeply intertwined with their faith. They believed that their faith was the bedrock upon which their enduring love was built.

Tom shared his thoughts on faith and love: "Faith is not just a part of our relationship; it's the foundation. It's what sustains our love and makes it unshakeable."

11.3. Love That Nurtures

Their love was not static but dynamic, constantly growing and nurturing their relationship. They believed in the power of love to support, encourage, and inspire each other.

Megan spoke about their nurturing love: "We see our love as a source of strength. It nurtures our relationship, helping us to become better individuals and a stronger couple."

11.4. A Legacy of Love

The group members understood that their love was a legacy they hoped to pass on to future generations. They believed that a love that never fades was a gift that would inspire others.

David expressed their legacy of love: "We want to leave a legacy of enduring love, one that will continue to inspire our children, grandchildren, and beyond. We hope they'll see the beauty of faith-centered love."

11.5. The Power of Grace

Grace played a pivotal role in their love. They recognized that extending grace to each other and seeking God's grace in their lives was essential to the perpetuity of their love.

Beth spoke about the role of grace: "Grace is the glue that holds our love together. It's a gift that we give each other every day, and it's a reminder of God's grace in our lives."

As they concluded their final chapter, the group members were filled with a deep sense of faith, love, and gratitude. Their journey had not just been a path of dating differently; it had been a journey of love that would never fade.

With faith as their foundation, love as their compass, and grace as their constant companion, they left their meeting, ready to continue their journey with the assurance that their love would be enduring and inspiring to others who sought a similar path of love and faith.

12

Forever Faithful

Title: Dating Differently: A Christian Approach

In the heart of Graceville, where love and faith were interwoven, the group of young Christians had completed their journey of dating differently. They had explored the principles, foundations, challenges, joys, reflections, and the enduring nature of their Christian approach to dating. Now, in their final chapter, they reflected on a love that would remain forever faithful.

12.1. Faithfulness to God

For these young Christians, faithfulness was not just a virtue within their relationships; it was their commitment to God. They recognized that their love was an expression of their faithfulness to the divine, an offering of their hearts to their Creator.

Emily spoke of this profound faithfulness: "Our love is an act of devotion to God. It's a promise to remain faithful to Him by living out the love He teaches us."

12.2. Faithfulness to Each Other

Their faithfulness extended to one another. They believed in the power of fidelity and commitment within their relationship. Their love was not just enduring, but forever faithful, bound by promises and trust.

Tom shared his thoughts on faithfulness in their relationship: "We made promises to each other, not just as partners, but as believers in Christ. Our faithfulness to each other is a testament to the love and commitment we share."

12.3. The Role of God's Grace

They recognized the role of God's grace in their faithfulness. They understood that it was not their strength alone but the grace of God that empowered them to remain faithful to each other and their faith.

Megan expressed the significance of God's grace: "God's grace sustains us, allowing us to be faithful even in the face of challenges. His grace is a constant reminder of His presence in our love."

12.4. A Legacy of Faithfulness

As they contemplated the future, the group members were aware of the legacy of faithfulness they were building. They understood that their relationship was a model of faithful love that they hoped would inspire others.

David shared their hope for a legacy of faithfulness: "We want our love to be a beacon, inspiring others to embrace a love that is not just enduring but forever faithful. We hope they'll see the beauty of living out a love that mirrors God's faithfulness."

12.5. Walking Forward in Faithfulness

As they left their final session, the group members walked forward with a sense of unwavering faithfulness. Their journey had not only been a path of dating differently but a journey of living out a love that was forever faithful.

With God as their anchor, faithfulness as their commitment, and grace as their companion, they embarked on the next chapter of their lives, ready to inspire others to embrace a similar path of faithfulness, enduring love, and devotion to God.

Book Summary: Dating Differently: A Christian Approach

Dating Differently: A Christian Approach is a profound exploration of a unique perspective on romantic relationships. Set in the heart of Graceville, a community where faith and love intersect, this book follows a group of young Christians who are committed to approaching dating through the lens of their Christian beliefs. This book takes readers on a journey through twelve chapters, each offering insights into the principles, foundations, challenges, joys, and reflections of their faith-centered approach to dating.

The journey begins with an introduction to the central theme of dating differently through a Christian perspective, emphasizing the importance of faith and the search for a God-centered partner. The first chapter delves into the significance of purity and integrity in relationships, setting the tone for the journey ahead.

As the chapters progress, readers are introduced to the principles of effective communication, shared values, spiritual growth, and how to overcome challenges in a God-centered relationship. The book provides practical advice on building a strong foundation for a faith-driven partnership and highlights the importance of accountability and support from a Christian community.

In the middle of the book, the unique challenges and joys of dating differently are explored. Readers gain insights into how cultural pressures, patience, and accountability play a role in their approach to relationships. The book emphasizes the fulfillment found in shared spiritual growth, the sense of purpose that arises from serving others, and the importance of their supportive Christian community.

The later chapters shift the focus to the practical aspects of maintaining a God-centered relationship, including making important life decisions, supporting each other's dreams and aspirations, and navigating life's challenges with grace. The group members share their personal experiences and wisdom about handling these complexities while remaining grounded in their faith.

The penultimate chapters reflect on the transformation and hope the group has found in their unique journey. They share a message of inspiration to others who may be considering a Christian approach to dating, encouraging them to explore this path and find the same fulfillment and depth in their relationships.

The final chapters highlight the enduring love, grace, faith, and service that their relationships are founded upon. They express their hopes to leave a legacy of love, faith, and service to inspire future generations to pursue similar faith-centered relationships.

Dating Differently: A Christian Approach serves as an inspirational guide for those seeking a more meaningful and faith-based approach to dating and love. Through the experiences, challenges, and joys of the group members, the book showcases the profound beauty of enduring love, faithfulness, and grace in the context of romantic relationships. It demonstrates that faith and love can serve as guiding lights in the journey of dating differently, ultimately leading to a life filled with purpose, faith, and love that never fades.

www.ingramcontent.com/pod-product-compliance
Lightning Source LLC
LaVergne TN
LVHW020456080526
838202LV00057B/5991